ARIES

HOROSCOPE

& ASTROLOGY

2023

Mystic Cat Publishing House

Suite 41906, 3/2237 Gold Coast HWY

Mermaid Beach, Queensland, 4218

Australia

www.Mystic-Cat.com

Contents

ARIES 2023
HOROSCOPE & ASTROLOGY

Four Weeks Per Month

Week 1 – Days 1 - 7

Week 2 – Days 8 - 14

Week 3 – Days 15 - 21

Week 4 – Days 22 – Month-end

ARIES

Aries Dates: March 21st to April 19th
Zodiac Symbol: Ram
Element: Fire
Planet: Mars
House: First
Colors: Red, white

2023 AT A GLANCE

Eclipses

Hybrid Solar - April 20th

Penumbral Lunar - May 5th

Annular Solar - October 14th

Partial Lunar -October 28th

Equinoxes and Solstices

Spring - March 20th 21:25

Summer - June 21st 14:52

Fall - September 23rd 06:50

Winter - December 22nd 03:28

Mercury Retrogrades

December 29th Capricorn - January 18th Capricorn

April 21st Taurus - May 15th Taurus

August 23rd Virgo - September 15th Virgo

December 13th Capricorn - January 2nd, Sagittarius

2023 FULL MOONS

Wolf Moon: January 6th 23:09

Snow Moon: February 13th, 18:30

Worm Moon March 7th, 12:40

Pink Moon: April 6th, 04:37

Flower Moon: May 5th, 17:34

Strawberry Moon: June 4th, 03:42

Buck Moon: July 3rd, 11:40

Sturgeon Moon: August 1st, 18:32

Blue Moon: August 31st, 01:36

Corn, Harvest Moon: September 29th, 06:50

Hunters Moon: October 28th, 20:23

Beaver Moon: November 27th, 09:16

Cold Moon: December 27th, 00:34

2023 INGRESSES

When a planet moves into a new sign or house of the zodiac, it ingresses into the next area. This planetary movement creates an energy shift that can affect your life on many levels. It changes the tone, flavor, and energetic expression of life. Changing cosmic alignments can have detrimental or beneficial impacts on your life.

Some celestial bodies change every few days, others every few weeks, a few only have changes occurring every few years. The longer the time interval between a planet's ingress, the slower the effect on your life.

Cosmic vibrations ripple around your energy field and help raise your vibration, or conversely, lower your energy. It brings a time of change that can affect your life on many levels. Being aware of upcoming changes helps you research and stay mindful of how planetary ingresses may affect your world.

Faster Moving Ingresses

Mar 25, 2023, 11:46	Mars enters Cancer
May 20, 2023, 15:32	Mars enters Leo
Jul 10, 2023, 11:41	Mars enters Virgo
Aug 27, 2023, 13:20	Mars enters Libra
Oct 12, 2023, 04:04	Mars enters Scorpio
Nov 24, 2023, 10:15	Mars enters Sagittarius

Faster Moving Ingresses

Jan 3, 2023, 02:10	Venus enters Aquarius
Jan 27, 2023, 02:33	Venus enters Pisces
Feb 20, 2023, 07:56	Venus enters Aries
Mar 16, 2023, 22:34	Venus enters Taurus
Apr 11, 2023, 04:48	Venus enters Gemini
May 7, 2023, 14:25	Venus enters Cancer
Jun 5, 2023, 13:47	Venus enters Leo
Oct 9, 2023, 01:11	Venus enters Virgo
Nov 8, 2023, 09:31	Venus enters Libra
Dec 4, 2023, 18:51	Venus enters Scorpio
Dec 29, 2023, 20:24	Venus enters Sagittarius

Faster Moving Ingresses

Feb 11, 2023, 11:23	Mercury enters Aquarius
Mar 2, 2023, 22:52	Mercury enters Pisces
Mar 19, 2023, 04:24	Mercury enters Aries
Apr 3, 2023, 16:22	Mercury enters Taurus
Jun 11, 2023, 10:27	Mercury enters Gemini
Jun 27, 2023, 00:24	Mercury enters Cancer
Jul 11, 2023, 04:11	Mercury enters Leo
Jul 28, 2023, 21:32	Mercury enters Virgo
Oct 5, 2023, 00:09	Mercury enters Libra
Oct 22, 2023, 06:49	Mercury enters Scorpio
Nov 10, 2023, 06:25	Mercury enters Sagittarius
Dec 1, 2023, 14:32	Mercury enters Capricorn

Slower Moving Ingresses

Mar 7, 2023, 13:35	Saturn enters Pisces
Mar 23, 2023, 12:14	Pluto enters Aquarius
May 16, 2023, 17:21	Jupiter enters Taurus

THE MOON PHASES

- New Moon (Dark Moon)
- Waxing Crescent Moon
- First Quarter Moon
- Waxing Gibbous Moon
- Full Moon
- Waning Gibbous (Disseminating) Moon
- Third (Last/Reconciling) Quarter Moon
- Waning Crescent (Balsamic) Moon

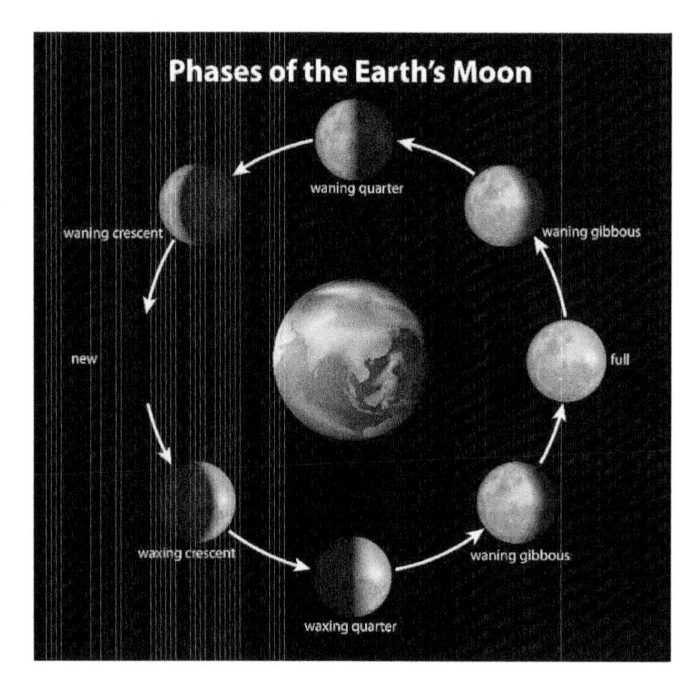

2023

JANUARY

M	T	W	T	F	S	S
						1
2	3	4	5	6	7	8
9	10	11	12	13	14	15
16	17	18	19	20	21	22
23	24	25	26	27	28	29
30	31					

FEBRUARY

M	T	W	T	F	S	S
		1	2	3	4	5
6	7	8	9	10	11	12
13	14	15	16	17	18	19
20	21	22	23	24	25	26
27	28					

MARCH

M	T	W	T	F	S	S
		1	2	3	4	5
6	7	8	9	10	11	12
13	14	15	16	17	18	19
20	21	22	23	24	25	26
27	28	29	30	31		

APRIL

M	T	W	T	F	S	S
					1	2
3	4	5	6	7	8	9
10	11	12	13	14	15	16
17	18	19	20	21	22	23
24	25	26	27	28	29	30

MAY

M	T	W	T	F	S	S
1	2	3	4	5	6	7
8	9	10	11	12	13	14
15	16	17	18	19	20	21
22	23	24	25	26	27	28
29	30	31				

JUNE

M	T	W	T	F	S	S
			1	2	3	4
5	6	7	8	9	10	11
12	13	14	15	16	17	18
19	20	21	22	23	24	25
26	27	28	29	30		

JULY

M	T	W	T	F	S	S
					1	2
3	4	5	6	7	8	9
10	11	12	13	14	15	16
17	18	19	20	21	22	23
24	25	26	27	28	29	30
31						

AUGUST

M	T	W	T	F	S	S
	1	2	3	4	5	6
7	8	9	10	11	12	13
14	15	16	17	18	19	20
21	22	23	24	25	26	27
28	29	30	31			

SEPTEMBER

M	T	W	T	F	S	S
				1	2	3
4	5	6	7	8	9	10
11	12	13	14	15	16	17
18	19	20	21	22	23	24
25	26	27	28	29	30	

OCTOBER

M	T	W	T	F	S	S
						1
2	3	4	5	6	7	8
9	10	11	12	13	14	15
16	17	18	19	20	21	22
23	24	25	26	27	28	29
30	31					

NOVEMBER

M	T	W	T	F	S	S
		1	2	3	4	5
6	7	8	9	10	11	12
13	14	15	16	17	18	19
20	21	22	23	24	25	26
27	28	29	30			

DECEMBER

M	T	W	T	F	S	S
				1	2	3
4	5	6	7	8	9	10
11	12	13	14	15	16	17
18	19	20	21	22	23	24
25	26	27	28	29	30	31

Time set to Coordinated Universal Time Zone

(UT±0)

Meteor Showers are on the date they peak.

JANUARY

Sun	Mon	Tue	Wed	Thu	Fri	Sat
1	2	3	4	5	6	7
8	9	10	11	12	13	14
15	16	17	18	19	20	21
22	23	24	25	26	27	28
29	30	31				

ASTROLOGY

January 3rd - Quadrantids Meteor Shower. Jan 1st-5th

January 6th - Wolf Moon. Full Moon in Cancer 23:09

January 7th - Mercury at Inferior Conjunction

January 12th - Mars Retrograde ends in Gemini

January 15th - Last Quarter Moon in Libra 02:10

January 18th - Mercury Retrograde ends in Capricorn

January 21st - New Moon in Aquarius 20:55

January 22nd - Uranus Retrograde ends in Taurus January 22nd - Chinese New Year (Rabbit)

January 28th - First Quarter Moon in Taurus 15:19

January 30th - Mercury at Greatest Elong: 25.0°W

NEW MOON

FULL MOON

JANUARY WEEK ONE

The Quadrantids Meteor Shower blazes across the night sky this week. A Full Moon in Cancer is perfect for renewing and rejuvenating your life from the ground up. As you find your balance in this ever-changing environment, you connect with new pathways that take you towards growth. Maintaining a flexible approach helps you adjust to the essential changes that grow your world in a new direction. A significant transformation takes place in your life; it offers a creative and therapeutic aspect.

You have been doing a fantastic job healing the past. A change of pace ahead gives you a chance to catch up with friends. It offers a brighter chapter that has you feeling connected, refreshed, and inspired. If you have felt adrift in life lately, connecting with your social tribe attracts support and friendship into your life.

A fortunate trend ahead nurtures your creativity and bolsters your mood. It helps you get established in an area with room to advance your talents and grow your abilities. It lets you integrate change sustainably in a grounded manner that grows your life and blesses your world. You may be questioning the path ahead, wondering what is next for your life. Indeed, examining your larger goals brings a journey worth exploring. Life picks up momentum and brings a refreshing change of pace. A new chapter head draws improvement and a sense of rejuvenation that nurtures new possibilities for your life.

JANUARY WEEK TWO

Mars retrograde ends in Gemini this week. Mars is the planet of desires, actions, energy, passion. You reveal a piece of the puzzle that gives insight into the path ahead. New options leave you feeling inspired and optimistic about the future. You reach a turning point and grow a journey that offers rising prospects for your life.

A fresh cycle beckons and brings excitement into your life. Expect developments ahead that attract new possibilities. It underscores an atmosphere of personal growth and self-development that aligns you with nurturing a journey that reflects the person you are becoming. Setting intentions provides a mix of manifestation that cracks the code to a brighter chapter. Working with your skills sharpens your talents and refines your abilities. It sparks new potential that advances life forward towards an enterprising area.

Something special makes a grand entrance into your life. It helps you reawaken to a sense of wonder as you establish your abilities in an area that offers creativity and progress. Your circumstances light up with refreshing options that place you towards growing your skills and expanding your talents. It marks an enriching journey that harnesses the essence of adventure as you head towards developing a way forward that holds meaning in your life. It becomes the gateway from which future growth occurs. An influx of creative options tempts you towards rising prospects.

JANUARY WEEK THREE

Mercury retrograde ends in Capricorn. A New Moon in Aquarius at week's end. An opportunity arrives soon, bringing a fresh wave of potential into your social life. It shines an illustrious light on nurturing companionship and friendship. News ahead draws excitement as plans take shape to mingle. It brings a spontaneous time of sharing with cohorts in an engaging and relaxing environment. Positive information on the horizon shines a light on expanding your circle of friends. A surge of well-being and potential hits the sweet note in your social life. It draws a cheerful time that nurtures interpersonal bonds. It brings solutions and offers a social aspect that attracts lively discussions.

Life heads to an upswing as a social invitation draws excitement. Embracing new possibilities offers a path that brings a journey worth growing. Sharing with friends nurtures well-being and cultivates rising creativity. Options pop up to support growing your world, and this openness you express takes you in a direction that draws abundance. The tides turn in your favor and bring lively discussions and social opportunities your way. You secure balanced foundations in a warm and lavish landscape. Enriching conversations blend ideas and help you craft beautiful plans. A time of growth and learning is ahead for your life. There is also a creative element that combines your innovation with aspirations. It allows you to reshape goals and plot a course towards your vision for future growth.

JANUARY WEEK FOUR

The Chinese New Year of the Rabbit represents fertility, luck, and growth. Being open to change places you in the proper alignment to progress your circumstances towards developing a new area. You make a decision that cracks the code to a brighter chapter. It emphasizes self-development and working with your skills and abilities to advance life forward towards greener pastures. It is a journey that aligns with the person you are becoming. News arrives that points you in the right direction.

A curious assignment ahead lights up growth, learning, and self-expression pathways. Your star is rising; continue to focus on developing your skills as progress is around the corner. As you connect with advancing life forward, you discover new responsibilities that draw growth and security into your world.

Creating space to nurture your abilities brings a path that aligns with your higher calling. Creating a sanctuary to nurture your talents draws balance and stability into your world. You unwrap a creative time that promotes inspiration and growth. Essential changes attract the correct type of people and opportunities into your life. You can expect increasing developments in the areas of personal growth and self-expression. The wheels are in motion to head towards rising prospects in your life. You build a firm foundation that draws stability in your world. You scoop the pull when you reveal a journey that offers room to progress your skills. An enterprising area comes calling, and it reflects your hopes and dreams.

FEBRUARY

Sun	Mon	Tue	Wed	Thu	Fri	Sat
			1	2	3	4
5	6	7	8	9	10	11
12	13	14	15	16	17	18
19	20	21	22	23	24	25
26	27	28				

ASTROLOGY

February 1st - Imbolc

February 5th - Snow Moon. Full Moon in Leo 18:30

February 13th - Last Quarter Moon in Scorpio 16:01

February 16th - Saturn in Conjunction with Sun

February 20th - New Moon in Pisces 07:08

February 27th - First Quarter Moon in Gemini 08:06

NEW MOON

FULL MOON

A Full Moon in Leo attracts a time of rejuvenation into your life that offers room to smooth out the rough edges. It helps you sweep away areas that are no longer relevant and move forward towards new possibilities. News arrives that brings a boost into your world. A situation you nurture takes on a life of its own and brings happiness into your life. It marks a time of renewal that underscores the energy of abundance.

You are in a time of transformation. It can feel challenging but rewards you with a breakthrough that nurtures creativity and helps you grow your life in a new direction. A gateway opens that gives you a joyous journey to channel your energy into development. A catalyst for change helps you discover those areas that offer the most incredible abundance in your world. Your willingness to be open to all types of possibilities draws a bountiful selection of options into your world.

Life is about to get busy; you can embrace the challenges ahead as they grow your experience and nurture a wellspring of potential in your life. An idea takes shape and crystallizes into a meaningful path forward for your life. It encourages you to take the plunge and dive into new territory that expands your horizons. It earmarks an exciting phase of change and discovery ahead. Moving onward brings improvement to your career path. Your confidence rises, enabling you to succeed as you extend your reach into a new area.

New options ahead encourage you to step out of your everyday routine and try new possibilities for your life. It opens a journey that activates new opportunities in your world. It places you in the proper alignment to broaden your circle of friends. Nurturing companionship in your life adds a valuable sense of security as it provides the grounded foundations and a balanced lifestyle. The changes ahead plant a new journey that nurtures well-being and promotes creativity. A landscape of green and lush possibilities weaves future dreams and goals.

It brings improvement into your home life as you get a glimpse of a compelling journey forward that offers a vibrant social aspect. Finding the missing element holds the key to future happiness. Expanding your circle of friends connects you with someone optimistic and joyful. It brings a shifting time where you focus on nurturing personal bonds.

Life showers a double dose of goodness over your situation. It brings a social aspect that offers entertaining discussions and a lively and vibrant atmosphere. A sense of celebration hangs in the air as you get busy catching up with friends and loved ones. Nurturing grounded foundations offers a boost that stabilizes and restores well-being and harmony. It lights a path forward to improving home and family life.

FEBRUARY WEEK THREE

A New Moon in Pisces draws a unique assignment into your life. Harnessing adaptability, flexibility, and innovation helps crack the code to a brighter chapter that connects you with kindred spirits. New information ahead stirs the pot of potential in your life and helps you manifest pleasing outcomes. It opens pathways that nurture social connection and expansion. Engaging with the broader world of possibility around your life shines a light on wellness and happiness. It refreshes and rejuvenates on many levels.

Life turns a corner and heads towards smoother sailing. The more perspective you gain into the path ahead, the more choices become available in your life. You guide your way forward and become comfortable with nurturing more excellent stability in your life. Re-evaluating priorities draws emotional realignment that facilitates a balanced landscape. It is constructive to set intentions and map out plans for future development this week.

A social aspect ahead nurtures bonds. Being open to new people helps you manifest a dream journey that draws happiness into your life. It highlights a time of freedom and adventure that strongly emphasizes developing your personal life. Engaging with areas that speak to your heart rebalances and rejuvenates your spirit. A unique aspect is coming that brings someone who shares thoughtful discussions and kind gestures.

FEBRUARY WEEK FOUR

An opportunity to socialize brings a breakthrough. It sends positive energy that raises confidence and has you merging thoughts with someone who feels compatible with your life. It spurs imagination and creativity, which offers self-expression and thoughtful discussions. Engaging talks offer companionship and nurture well-being and stability. It all adds to a prosperous and rejuvenating landscape ahead in your life.

A positive trend emerges that brings a busy time of shaping goals and launching your star higher towards a new vision. It brings an enterprising time that sees you tackling your goals with relish. Opportunities ahead expand your life and attract a pleasing outcome that rewards you on many levels. A forward-facing focus prevents back slides and helps you achieve the best results possible for your world.

Heightened opportunities ahead bring an active phase of growth and development into your life that lets you head towards an area of interest. Being open to new people and possibilities cranks up the potential possible. Focusing on developing your world brings the cream to the top. It offers a pleasing result that nurtures your abilities. It provides a lively and dynamic environment that brings moments to share with friends.

MARCH

Sun	Mon	Tue	Wed	Thu	Fri	Sat
			1	2	3	4
5	6	7	8	9	10	11
12	13	14	15	16	17	18
19	20	21	22	23	24	25
26	27	28	29	30	31	

March 7th - Worm Moon. Full Moon in Virgo 12:40

March 15th - Last Quarter Moon: Sagittarius 02:08
March 15th - Neptune in Conjunction with Sun

March 17th - Mercury at Superior Conjunction

March 20th - Ostara/Spring Equinox 21:25

March 21st - New Moon in Pisces 17:22

March 29th - First Quarter Moon in Cancer 02:32

NEW MOON

FULL MOON

MARCH WEEK ONE

A Full Moon in Virgo draws a time that reboots and rejuvenates the potential possible in your life. You fling the doors open to a social aspect when someone re-emerges to share news and conversations with you. It attracts the correct type of stability to grow your social life. It offers a richly creative process of lively discussions and thoughtful dialogues that nurture a wellspring of potential in your life. A changing environment ahead lights up new pathways of growth.

The Full Moon offers a way to reflect on the most meaningful areas in your life. It is a calling to focus on the foundations and build stability around your home life. Being proactive and grounding your energy in the regions that make you happy help release the tension. It does bring a new chapter into your life soon that washes away the stress and heads you towards rising prospects in your life.

Healing and nurturing your life are essential on many levels. Make yourself a priority; focus on the abundance ready to emerge in your world. Your willingness to persevere draws excellent possibilities to light that nurture your spirit. Rebalancing your energy by focusing on the basics in your life attracts harmony and happiness. News arrives that brings a boost of excitement this week.

MARCH WEEK TWO

You turn a corner soon and head towards greener pastures. Curious changes ahead shift your focus and bring new options to your table. It is a pivotal time that leads to change and discovery. Setting intentions and aspirations are essential in nurturing the essence of manifestation. Life showers new possibilities that enrich your world and bring an influx of growth to your door.

Life is ripe with possibility and potential as a fortune shines brightly over your life. Exploring options brings a fruitful time that develops a significant area. Growth and learning are at the crux of developing your abilities. Pushing back the barriers lets you secure rising prospects from which to grow your dreams. Channeling your energy into working with your talents ensures a pleasing result. It draws a time of change that connects with a breakthrough. New possibilities draw a surge of optimism that brings thoughtful conversations and a chance to share trailblazing ideas and thoughts. It translates to a fresh start that offers growth and stability. A potent mix of manifestation, inspiration, and intention will keep life busy.

Dabbling in your interests shines a light on nurturing creativity in your life. It secures foundations that draw stability and balance into your surroundings. Working with your gifts offers a calming influence that releases stress and nurtures well-being.

MARCH WEEK THREE

The Spring Equinox this week offers brilliance in your life. You soon discover an open road of potential comes calling. Being open to people and possibilities brings a time of nurturing your life. It opens an active chapter that lets you engage with a broader world of potential in your social life. Opportunity comes knocking, which helps you turn the page on a fresh growth cycle. Navigating an ever-changing environment with flexibility and adaptability lays the groundwork for solid foundations from which to grow your world outwardly.

Nurturing your home life brings notable changes that offer a path of growth and progression. It translates to a new chapter of possibility that promotes interpersonal bonds and brings a relaxed ambiance and thoughtful discussions to the forefront of your life. It jumpstarts an active time of open communication that improves the foundations in your life. It brings an engaging time that feels good for your soul.

Rising prospects ahead help you clear the slate and open a new road of potential in your life. Life is about to become busy as change is incoming, bringing the news, invitations, and leads into your life. A time of planning and growth will help you navigate the options and head towards developing your skills. It marks the start of something big in your life as it shines a light on an area worth your time. Harnessing the power of your vision raises confidence. It lets you take action to improve energy and progress your abilities forward.

MARCH WEEK FOUR

This week, Pluto lands in Aquarius, your third house of sharing, communication, and self-development. Pluto is the doorway through which volatile compressed pockets of self, spirit and primal energy lie hidden, which are released either by our efforts or by provocation from the outside world.

Remarkable opportunities for growth soon land in your lap. It cultivates an impressive journey that takes you towards greener pastures. Expanding your life and nurturing your abilities fortifies the foundations in your world. You connect with a unique crew of characters who grow your circle of friends. It offers trailblazing brainstorming times shared with kindred spirits who light up pathways of inspiration and creativity. A joint project or collaboration is earmarked for your life next year and is a source of pride in your life.

Things are ready to turn a corner in your life. Being open to new change and possibilities lets you break free from restrictive patterns that hold life back from reaching its highest destination. Self-discovery and personal growth become a focus as you move forward towards nurturing a meaningful area that breathes fresh air into your life. Creativity rises as you discover information that lets you transition into a new place of learning. Fanning the flames of your inspiration draws a busy time working with your talents.

APRIL

Sun	Mon	Tue	Wed	Thu	Fri	Sat
						1
2	3	4	5	6	7	8
9	10	11	12	13	14	15
16	17	18	19	20	21	22
23	24	25	26	27	28	29
30						

April 6th - Pink Moon. Full Moon in Libra 04:37

April 11th - Jupiter in Conjunction with Sun
April 11th - Mercury at Greatest Elong: 19.5°E

April 13th - Last Quarter Moon in Capricorn 09:11

April 20th - New Moon in Taurus 04:12
April 20th - Hybrid Solar Eclipse

April 21st - Mercury Retrograde begins in Taurus

April 22nd - Lyrids Meteor Shower. April 16-25

April 27th - First Quarter Moon in Leo 21:20

NEW MOON

FULL MOON

APRIL WEEK ONE

The Full Moon in Libra offers discovery on a personal level. Look for clues about the path ahead. New information is ready to surface, bringing a significant turning point into your life. You soon get the feeling that things are clicking into place as you reveal a new option that feels like the right fit for your life. It brings a unique path forward that lets you touch down on growing your life in a refreshing direction. It connects you with creative types who offer thoughtful discussions and supportive dialogues. You trigger a path of expanding opportunities by being open to change.

Being open to new possibilities washes away outworn energy and creates space to nurture a lighter atmosphere in your life. A whirlwind of activity overhead brings new dreams and goals into focus. Working with your creativity puts the icing on the cake as you discover a lead worth your time. It lifts the lid on an enterprising chapter that grows a path towards rising prospects.

Nurturing the foundations in your life draws a balanced and abundant landscape. It is natural and reasonable to feel anxious as you deal with uncertainties in your life. Focusing on the basics and nurturing your home life draws a solid foundation to grow your world. A new approach ahead draws lightness and happiness into your life. It brings a strong uptick of potential for your social life that connects you with companions who support and nurture your world. Sharing thoughtful discussions facilitates harmony.

APRIL WEEK TWO

Jupiter attracts good fortune and luck this week in conjunction with the Sun. A strong emphasis on improving the day-to-day running of your world launches improved stability. It nurtures a balanced and harmonious foundation in your life. It initiates positive growth that draws optimism and happiness into your life. Unique pathways ahead tempt you towards developing your talents. New friends enter your life which expands your circle of friends.

You soon touch down on an exciting path that develops your talents into a new area. It opens uncharted territory as you discover a gateway forward that grows your abilities. Expansion around your life promotes new goals and dreams. Life aligns favorably to upgrade your skills and develop your talents. Being open to change initiates a progression, growth, and evolution phase that offers an active and productive environment. It lets you sink your teeth into devouring a new area of interest as you get busy growing your world.

Being open to new possibilities offers your life some high-level options that help grow your world. It brings an end to postponements as you get busy developing your skills and nurturing your talents. Motivation and confidence rise as unique opportunities emerge that inspire new developments in your life. It brings an open road of possibilities that help you power through and head towards a brighter chapter.

APRIL WEEK THREE

A New Moon in Taurus at the week's end offers a time of planning and preparation for the coming month. Life becomes a blaze of new potential soon. Events line up to nourish your soul and nurture well-being in your life. Your willingness to work towards your dreams opens up to an abundant landscape that lets you create remarkable progress in your world. The way forward becomes bright and optimistic as you get a chance to rejuvenate life and nurture a wellspring of possibility.

New leads emerge that have you thinking about growth, learning, and advancement. A course or other learning possibility is a source of inspiration that helps break down barriers and lead you towards growth. It offers both challenges and progression for your life. Being open to possibilities advance life towards greener pastures. It brings a journey of self-development that lets you touch down on an ample time of growing dreams.

Life brings an opportunity to learn and prosper. Growing your abilities opens an expressive and expansive journey that nurtures your skills. You discover hidden pathways that hold curious options for your life. You soon create a bridge towards greener pastures that marks the start of growing your world. It brings a busy time that lets you embark on launching your talents higher.

Lyrids Meteor Shower helps you become in sync with your vision for future growth as it draws a better outcome for your career path. You uncover information that enables you to create exceptional progress. Well-crafted ideas are soon launched into the stratosphere, allowing you to develop your skills. Being open to side options helps develop unique goals that grow your abilities. Doing research and planning helps map out potential areas for development next year—life rewards on many levels as you uncover intriguing leads.

You soon get your bearings in a unique landscape of potential. It connects your life with an area worth growing. An undercurrent of change draws new adventures that offer liberation and expansion into your life. Pushing past perceived limitations reveals a unique possibility for your life.

Focusing on the building blocks of your life takes you towards a little worn track. This path nurtures your skills and elevates your abilities in a curious area. It helps you take the first steps on a journey that holds meaning. It gives you the green light to connect with inspiration and pour your energy into developing your talents. You soon attract abundance, which supports and sustains as you expand horizons and grow your life in a unique direction. Harnessing your creativity cracks the code to transform life as you develop new possibilities.

MAY

Sun	Mon	Tue	Wed	Thu	Fri	Sat
	1	2	3	4	5	6
7	8	9	10	11	12	13
14	15	16	17	18	19	20
21	22	23	24	25	26	27
28	29	30	31			

ASTROLOGY

May 1st - Mercury at Inferior Conjunction
May 1st Pluto retrograde begins in Aquarius

May 5th - Flower Moon. Full Moon in Scorpio 17:34
May 5th - Penumbral Lunar Eclipse

May 6th - Eta Aquarids Meteor Shower, April 19th - May 28th

May 9th - Uranus in Conjunction with Sun

May 12th - Last Quarter Moon in Aquarius 14:28

May 15th - Mercury Retrograde ends in Taurus

May 19th - New Moon in Taurus 15:54

May 27th - First Quarter Moon in Virgo 15:22

May 29th - Mercury at Greatest Elong: 24.9°W

NEW MOON

FULL MOON

Pluto's planet goes retrograde this week before a full Moon in Scorpio combines with a penumbral lunar eclipse. Limiting exposure to toxic environments and setting barriers around people who undermine your progress is a golden ticket towards improving your life. Making yourself a priority is essential in achieving happiness and harmony in your world. Staying true to your spirit lets you unearth new projects and unique prospects for your life. Being open to change and possibilities speaks volumes to the person you are now becoming.

Being open to change and exploring possibilities for your life helps you emerge from a quiet time and head towards growth. Pushing back the barriers lets you create tracks on growing your life and developing a journey that holds significant meaning to you. You can trust your instincts as you chase your dreams and forge a path forward. An area you create offers exciting prospects for your career path.

Experimenting and exploring the different options in your life brings new possibilities to light that help you achieve growth. Rising prospects ahead progress life forward into new areas. New goals combine with an inspiring vision that grows your life outwardly. A big reveal draws a sense of celebration and excitement as you connect with inspiration and unearth the right path forward for your life.

In conjunction with the Sun, Uranus shines a light on developing plans and placing your goals and dreams on the front burner; it sparks progression in your life. You attract something you have been seeking, and this draws a new cycle of potential into your life that takes your aspirations to the next level. It offers a sparkling path that promotes creative inspiration, freedom, and adventure. It places you in contact with kindred spirits, which lets you become proactively involved in developing your social life. Being open to change and possibility is the catalyst for growth that sparks a whirlwind of activity.

Future planning enables you to create progress in your life. Preparing to embark on new adventures allows you to climb the ladder and head towards successful horizons. Being a pioneer offers a unique approach that lets you diverge from your usual routine and expand your life in a new direction. Creativity rises as promising leads ahead nurture inspiration. Stepping out of your comfort zone opens your life up to new people and experiences. You soon be able to develop your talents and grow your skills. With careful planning and a sound, thought-out approach, you set yourself up for a higher level of success in your life. It brings decisions and choices that help shape the path ahead. Capitalizing on opportunities keep life dynamic and vibrant as you evolve your abilities and head towards greener pastures.

Mercury retrograde ends in Taurus and an area you nurture blossoms and draw ample time for soul-stirring conversations that feel good for your mood. Sharing with kindred spirits leaves you feeling empowered and ready to tackle unique projects. It brings a time of creativity and innovation to build your talents and advance your abilities. It marks a significant chapter that becomes the gateway to growing your life. You get wind of some curious information that unlocks an enriching journey. Change surrounds your life on many levels and orients you towards rising prospects.

You make notable tracks on improving your situation as you transition towards new possibilities that encourage growth. Learning new areas lifts the lid on rising prospects that inspire a journey towards greener pastures. It puts you in sync with unique options that offer advancement. Refining your skills facilitates high-level possibilities that provide a rich landscape for your creativity and talents.

A blank canvas of new options tempts you towards developing your creativity in a unique area. It opens a path that grows your world and improves the foundations in your life. Effectively channeling your energy into creating your dreams brings a turning point that offers room to advance your talents. It brings a journey that is inspiring, thought-provoking, and trailblazing. The atmosphere of abundance draws rising confidence which attracts new friends and companions.

New information arrives to crack the code to a brighter chapter in your life. It opens the door to a fresh start that marks a new beginning in your world. It offers a chance to progress your talents into an area that shows promise. It helps you stretch past your comfort zone and grow your abilities. It brings a unique endeavor to light that offers your skills to a broader audience. Taking your talents towards advancement draws an optimistic path forward. Life picks up the pace and offers kinship, growth, and expansion.

Advancement ahead progresses your talents into a new area. By being proactive, you create a gateway that advances your abilities. It sparks a productive chapter that ensures you are kept inspired and busy. Refining skills triggers a path that offers new options that grow your life exponentially as a surge of potential comes calling to take your talents to the next level. It connects you with others who share compatible interests and creativity. Refining your talents and creative skills opens the floodgates of rising potential in your life.

A new start flows into your life; it shines a light on a productive time that creates a strong basis for developing new goals and dreams. Creativity leads the way forward towards a vital shift that offers expansion in your social life. It connects you with kindred spirits who nurture an abundant landscape. Sharing your ideas with a tribe of creative people promotes a supportive environment.

JUNE

Sun	Mon	Tue	Wed	Thu	Fri	Sat
				1	2	3
4	5	6	7	8	9	10
11	12	13	14	15	16	17
18	19	20	21	22	23	24
25	26	27	28	29	30	

ASTROLOGY

June 4th - Strawberry Full Moon: Sagittarius 03:42
June 4th - Venus at Greatest Elong: 45.4°E

June 10th - Last Quarter Moon in Pisces 19:31

June 17th - Saturn Retrograde begins in Pisces

June 18th - New Moon in Cancer 04:38

June 21st - Midsummer/Litha Solstice 14:52

June 26th - First Quarter Moon in Libra 07:50

June 30th - Neptune Retrograde begins in Pisces

NEW MOON

FULL MOON

Venus reaches the greatest elongation as a full Moon in Sagittarius blooms. A sentimental theme reverberates around your life to help heal the past on an emotional level. Revisiting the past attracts treasured and meaningful memories into your spirit. It cultivates a balanced and warm chapter of reliving simple joys and feeling nostalgic. Reminiscing enables you to process outworn energy and release any difficult emotions clinging to your spirit. Reviewing your life on a deeper level brings insight into your life. If you feel the pain of regret or wash over you, releasing its hold on your emotions, clean the slate and prepare you to embark on a fresh chapter of potential. Understanding past lessons hold the key to future growth in your personal life. New options emerge after a time of healing and introspection. Listening to helpful advice is supportive and nurtures your energy as you lean into a time of advanced growth. Being open to change underscores your willingness to improve your circumstances by the choices and decisions you make for your life.

Many changes around your life help you improve your bottom line. It offers new possibilities and generates a great deal of forwarding momentum in your life. You shift away from outworn areas and discover the hidden blessings in learning and advancing your talents. Being proactive draws dividends as you climb the ladder to a new level of success in your working life. As you zoom towards new possibilities, you open a prosperous path ahead.

JUNE WEEK TWO

With Pluto landing in your tenth house of ambition, and motivation, expect to see advancement around your career path moving forward. Work-related opportunities crop up to inspire change. It does involve a degree of research and planning. Exploring options lets you blaze a trail towards rising prospects. Imaginative and creative possibilities nurture inspiration. The path ahead speeds up and draws a time of growth and expansion. It does see things are moving along for your working life. Advancing your vision forward seals the deal on a productive chapter ahead.

An intense concentration on developing your goals sparks a great deal of growth in your life. You direct your attention to a journey that advances your talents and refines your abilities. Working on your plan for the future gets everything ready to launch. Making tweaks and refinements is instrumental in drawing the best results possible. Your flexibility and creativity are valuable tools that help you chart a course towards achieving your dreams. New options ahead offer a rising aspect that nurtures your life on many levels. Rising prospects improve your bottom line, securing advancement for your working goals. It does bring opportunities to expand your career path. It is a time that grows your world outwardly. It lets you find balance while moving forward towards your goals. It does bring new challenges that see you working effectively with your talents to clear the path ahead.

JUNE WEEK THREE

The New Moon in Cancer before Midsummer/Litha Solstice at week's end. You reveal an exciting lead that broadens your horizons. Nurturing your talents attracts a greater degree of happiness and success into your life. Getting involved with a unique and lively area builds secure foundations that offer a vibrant time to cultivate your abilities. It promotes being adaptive, adventurous, and creative. A purposeful push towards developing your goals brings a pleasing result to light.

An emphasis on improving your circumstances helps you touch down on new possibilities for your social life. It illuminates a journey of increasing abundance, happiness, and companionship. It opens the gate to a lively environment that connects with your broader circle of friends. A positive ripple effect reverberates around your life, creating waves of new potential that mark a time of building grounded foundations in your world. It connects with people who share similar interests and goals. You develop supportive bonds with those who resonate on a similar wavelength.

Positive news arrives that shines a light on what you can achieve when exploring diverse growth pathways. Taking a courageous step towards learning a unique area brings a time of new beginnings that expands your life. It charts a course towards an enriching chapter that ushers in social engagement, laughter, and thoughtful discussions.

JUNE WEEK FOUR

The planet Neptune goes retrograde in Pisces. This planetary phase does an excellent job of dispelling illusions that could be holding your progress back from achieving your best. A new chapter draws beneficial options into your life, giving you a brighter picture of possibilities when you stay open to curious leads. Improvement is at the crux of the changes ahead. A lively and productive pathway launches an exciting direction that brings change and opportunity into your world. Something special makes a grand entrance that kicks off a journey of inspiration and exhilaration. It gets a chance to take on new endeavors that stimulate creativity and cultivate your talents. It draws an enterprising time of learning, growth, and productivity.

You enter a new chapter that offers progress, recognition, and advancement. You receive an acknowledgment, and this validation raises confidence and nurtures pride as you feel rewarded for your efforts. You reach an essential milestone in your career path that offers a successful outcome for your working life. Minimizing distractions and developing your goals provide a pleasing result for your life. You garner the attention of others who praise and compliment your efforts. This positive attention brings a boost into your world. It offers a supportive environment that lets you feel you are making a difference as you turn a corner and head towards growth and prosperity.

JULY

Sun	Mon	Tue	Wed	Thu	Fri	Sat
						1
2	3	4	5	6	7	8
9	10	11	12	13	14	15
16	17	18	19	20	21	22
23	24	25	26	27	28	29
30	31					

ASTROLOGY

July 1st - Mercury at Superior Conjunction

July 3rd - Buck Moon. Full Moon in Capricorn. Supermoon 11:40

July 10th - Last Quarter Moon in Aries 01:48

July 17th - New Moon in Cancer 18:32

July 23rd - Venus retrograde begins in Leo

July 25th - First Quarter Moon in Libra 22:06

July 28th - Delta Aquarids Meteor Shower. July 12th - August 23rd

NEW MOON

FULL MOON

JULY WEEK ONE

The Mercury at Superior conjunction. Full Moon in Capricorn, Supermoon. The past has grown your life experience in so many ways. It shapes the person you are today as you incorporate the lessons learned in your current situation. Indeed, new opportunities are incoming that take your talents to the next level. Streamlining and refining the path ahead offers a productive and growth-orientated journey that elevates your abilities. Creativity and inspiration raise the bar of what is possible in your life when you stay open to new options and possibilities. Nurturing your abilities draws an abundant landscape that enables you to gain traction on advancing energy forward. It seals the lid on a problematic chapter that feels finished. You get busy and embark on growing your world in a unique and inspiring direction.

Distancing drama and rebooting your life create foundations that harmonize and enrich your world. Being proactive about creating change in your life lets you go after your dreams and make your goals a priority. Advancement is in the pipeline; a new initiative comes calling and brings excitement into your world. A group enterprise with kindred spirits gets you involved with growing a journey of meaning and connection. Embracing life-affirming activities secures a stable and peaceful environment. It creates solid foundations from which to expand your world.

JULY WEEK TWO

Life picks up the pace and becomes more active and engaging. It lets you slide into a season of growth and expansion for your social life. Confidence rises and lights a path towards developing companionship. Opportunities to connect with your broader circle of friends bring optimism, drive, and happiness into your world. An influx of communication triggers an invitation to mingle. It connects you with sharing thoughts and ideas with friends who understand your personality and get your way of thinking. A self-expressive chapter ahead brings fun and friendship.

Events on the horizon beautifully support growth and expansion in your life. It offers you a peek into curious pathways that nurture talents and grow your abilities. Being open to new experiences shifts your life towards refreshing options. You can approach the path ahead like a tourist, sampling various options and nurturing unique adventures in your life. As you gain insight into the areas that spark your inspiration the most, you discover a greater sense of life purpose guiding you forward. Following your intuition offers a journey that enriches your life.

A fresh start flows into your life and brings a time driven by growth and expansion. It places you in the correct alignment to improve your circumstances. It is currently an ideal time for setting intentions and planning goals. Directing your energy towards developing dreams offers new adventures that cultivate rising prospects.

JULY WEEK THREE

This week a New Moon in Cancer connects you with an enterprising time that boosts your abilities. It provides a positive step in the right direction as an emphasis on growing your life offers advancement. Opportunities to improve life draw stability and growth. Rising prospects open up new leads to refine your skills and develop your talents.

Being receptive to change sparks your creativity and attracts new options into your life. Something around the corner brings a burst of inspiration that motivates you to grow your abilities and head towards unique pathways that offer growth and improvement. Nurturing your life provides an enriching journey that builds stable foundations and attracts well-being and happiness into your life. You open your world up to new adventures that let you set sail towards developing your dreams. Information ahead lights up excitement across the board.

Welcome news brings a boost into your life. It helps you break fresh ground as you create space to nurture new goals and possibilities for your life. Movement and discovery ahead offer growth opportunities. Working with your talents and evolving your gifts is part of a more expansive journey for your life that offers advancement and refinement. It opens up a path that grows your experience and gives you a real sense of gaining traction on your goals. You get involved with an expressive pursuit that inspires you creatively.

JULY WEEK FOUR

Venus retrograde begins in Leo, which can put a damper on developing your love life for the next little while. You may feel that things are slowing down, but it opens pathways that see you engaging in hobbies and interests. It draws a productive time for working with your talents, advancing your abilities towards new areas. You soon unveil thought-provoking possibilities. It brings a slower pace that helps you connect with the building blocks of your life. Life takes on a more meandering pace as you settle into an abundant landscape of possibilities. Tweaking plans, streamlining the path ahead lets you be effective and efficient as you plot a course towards developing new goals and areas. Slowing down brings heightened perspective; it draws rejuvenation and renewal. You soon feel refreshed and ready to focus on improving the potential that seeks expression in your world.

Using this time wisely to plan brings new options to light. It enables you to bridge the gap between where you are now and where you seek to climb in your life. It brings a landscape of lush green potential into your surroundings. You move towards a journey with unique possibilities that offer stable foundations and rising prospects. It kickstarts a cycle that rejuvenates and renews inspiration. Clear skies provide a sunny aspect that opens a pathway forward, connecting to increasing creativity.

AUGUST

Sun	Mon	Tue	Wed	Thu	Fri	Sat
		1	2	3	4	5
6	7	8	9	10	11	12
13	14	15	16	17	18	19
20	21	22	23	24	25	26
27	28	29	30	31		

August 1st - Full Sturgeon Moon in Aquarius Supermoon 18:32

August 8th - Last Quarter Moon in Taurus 10:28

August 10th - Mercury at Greatest Elong: 27.4°E

August 12th - Perseids Meteor Shower July 17th - Aug 24th

August 16th - New Moon in Leo 09:37

August 23rd - Mercury Retrograde begins in Virgo

August 24th - First Quarter Moon in Sagittarius 09:57

August 27th - Saturn at Opposition

August 29th - Uranus Retrograde begins in Taurus

August 31st - Full Moon, Supermoon, Blue Moon in Pisces 01:36

NEW MOON

FULL MOON

Full Moon, Supermoon in Aquarius attracts a light bulb moment that revolutionizes the potential possible in your world. You may be feeling delicate at this juncture. The Supermoon provides illumination, which guides you to look within and see what areas can be released. Taking time to focus on self-care and healing is therapeutic. It draws stability to your foundations, which helps begin a new journey for you to explore. Essential changes enable you to create space to improve your surroundings while keeping an eye open to new possibilities that draw expansion

Change is ready to flow into your world soon. It wipes the slate clean and brings a healing essence that helps you remove the worn layers. You yield a sense of stability that is rejuvenating. Good news is ahead that brings extra support into your world. Amid this time of shifting sands, you discover an area that calls your name. It lets you make strides towards building stable foundations.

Hidden messages appear in your everyday life to guide your path forward. Looking out for signs and symbols that spark your intuition brings essential information to light. Under this influence, your vision takes shape, and it offers a path of learning and growth to take your abilities to the next level. It brings an active and effective environment for growing your skills and exploring new pathways that crop up along the way.

Perseids meteor shower triggers inspiration. The more you engage with growing your world, the happier and more expansive it becomes. Fortune aligns to form a clear window of opportunity that expands life forward. Progression is surprisingly swift as advancement comes calling. It takes you on a purposeful journey that offers a slow but steady transformation. Plotting a course towards developing new goals fosters enriching moments. Staying open to new options brings an enterprise that feeds your creativity and grows your talents. It brings sweeping changes into your world that are part of your evolution.

Life heads to an upswing as you discover options that improve your world's bottom line. You land in a settled and grounded environment that sparks creative possibilities. It connects you with a journey that has you feeling optimistic about the prospects possible in your world. Expansion ahead brings options that grow the path. It sees you drifting away from distractions and focusing on a journey that holds meaning. Being proactive kickstarts growth and brings a positive trend that offers progress and success. Creative energy is rising, which fires up your inspiration. You are doing the right thing by exploring new possibilities for your life. Valuable rewards are on offer if you stay focused and grow your world. Information arrives that helps you build something tangible and concrete.

The new Moon in Leo brings fresh energy into your career path. A new role on offer takes your goals to the next level. Better conditions grow the stability in your life. Fine-tuning your talents does increase your mastery and opens new career path possibilities. It brings a productive time that offers a potent brew of potential. Being receptive to change helps you make the most of growing your skills.

Evaluating options takes you towards a new chapter that has you feeling excited about the possibilities in your life. Planning and developing future goals lets you stake your claim on improving your life as it gives you the green light to make yourself a priority. An emphasis on enhancing your circumstances attracts a valuable result. It transitions you to new options that encourage growth and learning. It increases your skills and deepens your understanding of the path ahead. It leads to a busy time of gaining new skills that offer advancement.

The path ahead clears. Indeed, being receptive to change lets you take advantage of expansive options overhead. It allows your talents to shine under sunny skies. It brings a purposeful and innovative path that advances your abilities and refines your skills. It helps you extend your reach and unearth new possibilities that improve the stability in your world.

AUGUST WEEK FOUR

Uranus retrograde begins in Taurus. Full Moon, Supermoon, Blue Moon in Pisces on the last day of the month. You face a crossroads, and this brings change. It does draw a reflective and introspective chapter as you contemplate the path ahead. You make a decision that brings a turning point. It liberates the tension and attracts abundance and social support. It does trigger a new chapter for your social life that draws the opportunity to nurture a bond. It brings a path that tempts you forward and enriches your life.

You reveal information that charms and inspires. It lets you make headway on expanding your social life. It brings an adventure-driven chapter that moves you out of your comfort zone and lets you mingle. It does seem that change is surrounding your environment; someone seeks to become closer. It does light a path towards abundance.

News is imminent; it provides a new option. The wheels are in motion to move away from situations that limit your potential. It is a time of growth that brings insight into pathways forward. It offers room to grow your social life; you are on the right track towards improving your circumstances. Connecting with a broader range of people brings the chance to nurture friendships and draw enrichment into your social life. It does see you spending more time with friends and companions. It does get a time that draws new people into your world.

SEPTEMBER

Sun	Mon	Tue	Wed	Thu	Fri	Sat
					1	2
3	4	5	6	7	8	9
10	11	12	13	14	15	16
17	18	19	20	21	22	23
24	25	26	27	28	29	30

September 4th - Venus Retrograde ends in Leo
September 4th - Jupiter Retrograde begins Taurus

September 6th - Last Quarter Moon in Gemini 22:21
September 6th - Mercury at Inferior Conjunction

September 15th - New Moon in Virgo 01:40
September 15th - Mercury Retrograde ends in Virgo

September 19th - Neptune at Opposition

September 22nd - Mercury at Greatest Elong 17.9°W
September 22nd - First Quarter Moon Sagittarius 19:32

September 23rd - Mabon/Fall Equinox. 06:50

September 29th - Corn Moon. Harvest Full Moon. Supermoon in Aries 09:58

NEW MOON

FULL MOON

SEPTEMBER WEEK ONE

Venus turns direct in Leo as Jupiter retrograde begins in Taurus. Your love life heats up when new energy brings a focus on communication and sharing. It offers excitement and romance as an active and dynamic environment fuels the desire to bond. It brings the room to nurture your personal life, and as Venus turns direct, it inspires growth and harmony in your world. It offers a gateway towards a happy chapter that brims with lively dialogues and entertaining discussions. It helps you remove the outworn layers that limit progress as you get involved with growing your life in a connected and happy fashion.

You connect with someone who draws emotional fulfillment and romance into your world. Rising prospects in your love life bring a new journey forward for your personal life. Open communication encourages a blissful and expansive environment for developing romance in your life. It soon triggers rising prospects in your social life that cultivate an abundant landscape of potential. It brings a time of chasing dreams and developing goals with someone who offers companionship. As the axis of your social life shifts, it draws your attention towards nurturing a bond that cracks the code to an abundant future. Serendipity lights the path forward, bringing an uptick of potential into your personal life. Constructive conversations reveal a great time you can cherish.

SEPTEMBER WEEK TWO

Little goes under your radar when you spot an opportunity to improve your circumstances. It brings advancement that lets you appreciate the path forward. An insightful person offers guidance and advice. This information is a game-changer; it points to a journey of change, progression, and growth. New opportunities are around your life, landing you in an environment ripe for advancement.

It is a time where the decisions made shape your destiny. It's an environment where you can let go of the past, wipe the slate clean, and turn the page on a new chapter of life. Growth arrives in unexpected ways, stirring up the winds of change. It brings a positive chapter with room to flex your social muscle with kindred spirits. It brings a wave of potential into your social life.

Life picks up and becomes more active and productive when news arrives that tempts you into a social environment. Spending time with friends in a community environment brings vital energy. It activates creativity and draws wellness into your spirit. It brings opportunities to share ideas and thoughts with others. It's an indication that you are ready to open your life to new people and experiences. It has you chasing leads and staying busy. An invitation ahead inspires your mind and has you thinking about the possibilities. It draws new pathways that advance your life forward. It helps you remove blocks and open the path ahead.

A New Moon in Virgo combines with Mercury retrograde ending this week. The changes ahead bring a time to shine. It lets you bid farewell to past issues that have blocked progress. It brings new possibilities that allow you to reach a turning point. An expansive landscape comes into view. It brings social opportunities that add richness to your life. It offers a powerful new beginning as it draws a fresh start into your social life. Lively conversations fuel a desire for expansion.

A positive trend ahead brings a happy influence into your world. It gets a chance to socialize with new people. It brightens your life with a time of mingling and fun. Sharing thoughts and ideas light a creative and artistic aspect that heightens innovative thinking. Brainstorming cracks the code to expand the potential in your life. It opens pathways that offer handsome returns on your time and energy. You unpack a stellar phase of new possibilities ahead.

You have a golden touch for anything you turn your hand to at this time. It draws a pleasing outcome is that gets you on track to expand horizons into new areas. Struggles fade away as a brilliant aspect arrives to tempt you forward. It offers a social path and a chance for collaboration with a kindred spirit. Lively discussions and constructive dialogues paint a broader picture of what is possible in your life when you link up with other creative characters. It does have you dreaming big about future possibilities and planning for future growth.

SEPTEMBER WEEK FOUR

Mabon/Fall Equinox occurs this week with a Full Moon. The Supermoon in Aries towards the week's end offers a changing landscape that draws healing; it provides a gateway towards a clean slate of potential. Being open to change underscores your willingness to improve your circumstances by engaging with your life and chasing those important leads that lead to growth. It helps advance life forward by removing the blocks that keep you stuck.

You enter a time that brings understanding into your life, nurturing grounded energy that draws healing. Your top priorities are peace, serenity, and stability. Focusing on the basics illustrates a new flow of energy into your environment. It lets things settle down as you pick up the pieces and begin to progress forward. It brings a spiritual journey into focus that helps rejuvenate your energy and release the pain.

A theme of closure and release draws healing. Banishing the clouds create space to pivot towards a happier chapter; it transitions you towards new possibilities that offer increasing potential. You move away from problems and embrace a newfound sense of belonging. Unlocking the key to your creativity sees your ideas spreading like wildfire. It helps you unleash your abilities into an exciting area that tips the scales in your favor. It puts you in contact with like-minded people who bring a sense of community and harmony into your world that is refreshing.

OCTOBER

Sun	Mon	Tue	Wed	Thu	Fri	Sat
1	2	3	4	5	6	7
8	9	10	11	12	13	14
15	16	17	18	19	20	21
22	23	24	25	26	27	28
29	30	31				

October 6th - Last Quarter Moon in Cancer 13.48

October 7th - Draconids Meteor Shower. Oct 6th-10th

October 11th - Pluto Retrograde ends in Capricorn

October 14th - New Moon in Libra 17:54
October 14th - Annular Solar Eclipse 17:59

October 20th - Mercury at Superior Conjunction

October 21st -Orionids Meteor Shower. Oct 2nd – Nov 7th

October 22nd - First Quarter Moon Aquarius 03.29

October 23rd - Venus at Greatest Elong: 46.4°W

October 28th - Partial Lunar Eclipse 20:14
October 28th - Hunters Full Moon in Taurus 20:23

NEW MOON

FULL MOON

Important news emerges that connects with a fruitful chapter of growth. It underpins advancement for your working life. It lets you exceed your current expectations and head towards rising prospects. Taking advantage of career opportunities ahead links you with a lead that generates excitement and success. It offers room to grow and prosper as you embark on a journey of developing your goals. Reshuffling the decks of fate brings a pursuit that takes your talents to the next level. It lets you harness your creativity to express your abilities and share your skills with a broader audience.

Serendipity lights the path forward. It gets a change of pace that has you working towards a new vision. It brings a high volume of new options to contemplate that transition you towards a fantastic assignment. A curious area calls your name and may dominate your thinking over the coming weeks. It sets you up to progress life forward into new areas, bringing all the abundance and happiness available to you at this time. You ride a wave of inspiration that carries you along as you enter a full-time for progression. It opens the gate to a prosperous cycle. Suppose you have drifted off course recently and are currently unsure of the correct direction to take. In that case, information flows freely into your life to give you a comprehensive view of the path ahead. Being focused helps you spot an area that holds water, and it highlights expansively growing your life. A positive trend takes your vision to new heights.

OCTOBER WEEK TWO

Pluto retrograde ends in Capricorn. New Moon in Libra at the week's end combines with an annular solar eclipse. Mapping out future goals for your life helps you discover further options for growth. Change is in the air; a fresh wind of potential arrives to stir things up in your social life. It connects you with creative people who offer a more connected support network. Combining thoughts and ideas with a crew of kindred spirits helps you blaze a trail towards developing new goals and projects. The essence of manifestation raises the bar as an influx of possibility tempts you forward. Your willingness to be open to new people and possibilities lets you set sail on calmer seas.

It brings a busy time that sparks adaptability and new adventures. As inspiration rises, it offers a peak time for creativity, drawing unique growth pathways. You discover an assignment that promotes your talents and allows your gifts to shine. It lets you dive into developing projects that offer growth and expand your abilities into new areas. A group environment shared with other trailblazers sparks a strong foundation for joint endeavors and collaborations.

Your patience and perseverance draw improvement into your life, offering more options to grow your life. You soon discover that more stability in your situation provides solid foundations that improve your circumstances. The more you explore various possibilities, the more you connect with your intuition and instincts to guide the path ahead.

Mercury at Superior conjunction brings an influx of inspiration, motivation, and drive into your life this week. Being open to new possibilities supports high-level options. It brings an end to postponements and delays for your career path. Doing research and exploring pathways draw improvement to your career sector. Your talents take center stage, and you soon get an idea that things will work in your favor. Mercury gives you newfound energy and courage to grow your life and extend your reach into a unique area.

New information kicks off a more social aspect that allows you to circulate more often with friends. A change of pace and environment ahead offers a brighter chapter that leaves you feeling optimistic about the potential possible in your world. Your creativity and inspiration burn brightly, opening up a treasure box of potential pathways. It brings a time of planning and developing your dreams and aspirations. Inspiring conversations with thoughtful companions nurture well-being and lead to happiness in your social life. Changes in your broader social environment help leave behind issues and drama. It brings an exciting chapter of lively discussions and thoughtful dialogues. It brings the spirit of adventure and freedom into focus as you connect with kindred spirits and enjoy some well-earned downtime. Replenishing your emotional tanks stabilizes foundations and opens the page to a new chapter in your book of life. A new project ahead brings excitement into view.

OCTOBER WEEK FOUR

This week, a partial lunar eclipse blends magic with a Full Moon in Taurus. A fantastic time of abundance and magic reinvents the potential possible in your social life. Surprise communication arrives out of the left-field. It brings the chance to deepen a friendship as it shines a potent light on personal goals. It fuels an exciting chapter of sharing thoughtful dialogues and insightful conversations. It brings liberation, freedom, and expansion into your social life. It is trusting instincts that guide you correctly.

Changes in the air and exploring a community setting with friends and companions nurtures well-being and harmony. It opens the door to a fresh start that paves the way towards a more connected environment. Thoughtful discussions and insightful conversations stir the pot of manifestation in your world. It brings ideas and options that grow your world outwardly.

Good fortune flows in and finds its level of happiness and harmony. Stabilizing foundations lets you make headway towards improving circumstances. It draws a therapeutic aspect as it nurtures well-being and peace. It lifts the lid on a forward-facing aspect that brings news and information into your life. It offers a social element that rejuvenates foundations and draws abundance into your world. It brings new goals and possibilities to light that enrich your life.

NOVEMBER

Sun	Mon	Tue	Wed	Thu	Fri	Sat
			1	2	3	4
5	6	7	8	9	10	11
12	13	14	15	16	17	18
19	20	21	22	23	24	25
26	27	28	29	30		

November 3rd - Jupiter at Opposition

November 4th - Saturn Retrograde ends in Pisces

November 4th - Taurids Meteor Shower.Sept 7th - Dec 10th

November 5th - Last Quarter Moon in Leo 08:37

November 13th - Uranus at Opposition
November 13th - New Moon in Scorpio 09:27

November 17th - Leonids Meteor Shower Nov 6th -30th

November 18th - Mars in Conjunction with Sun

November 20th - First Quarter Moon in Aquarius 10.50

November 27th – Beaver Moon. Full Moon in Gemini 09:16

NEW MOON

FULL MOON

Jupiter at opposition. Saturn retrograde ends in Pisces. With Saturn turning direct, it's full steam ahead for your career goals. The upside of this time is personal growth that encourages you to train or upskill in a new area. If you sabotage your ability to create security in your life, being open to a broader range of possibilities brings new growth. You can nurture a journey that blossoms into a dynamic path forward. Researching leads helps end difficulties that bring a sense of lack into your life. Addressing the limitations that hold you back from excelling in your working life opens up new pathways that take you towards rising prospects in your career.

Evaluating your goals and reflecting on your progress to date ensure you make the right choices and decisions ahead for your career path. Exploring leads bring a time of planning and preparation that advances your life forward. Looking at the bigger picture helps you discover an option that offers growth and prosperity in your career. After perseverance and waiting, you find an open road of potential that lets you get busy developing your working life. A new role enables you to taste the sweet flavor of success. Setting clear intentions, taking an active part in transforming your life allow you to navigate the path ahead with confidence and capability. Your intelligent choices and decisions pay off with a successful working life.

NOVEMBER WEEK TWO

The planet Uranus is in opposition as the New Moon occurs in Scorpio. Your patience and perseverance win out a pleasing result for your career path. Despite setbacks, your refusal to give up on your dreams draws a successful outcome into your life. Pushing forward against the flow of additional challenges takes courage, conviction, and determination. It brings the journey's final leg before you reach a lofty goal. An increasing workload tests your resolve before you get to the finishing line. Continuing despite weariness and fatigue opens up a new level of achievement in your studies. You find the inner resources necessary to overcome obstacles and reach your goals. Working towards your plan help you prosper as you maintain a steady focus and work towards your vision for future growth.

Change surrounds your world and brings forward progress that enables you to chase a dream you've had in the back of your mind for some time. It offers a breakthrough that triggers new possibilities and options for your life. The path ahead suddenly opens and leads to developing your life in a curious direction. It opens the floodgates to unique options that offer an enterprising avenue forward. It brings a productive chapter of working towards your goals. Ambition rises and brings an energizing chapter ahead. It creates progress that inspires and motivates growth.

Leonids Meteor Shower. Mars in conjunction with the Sun. You identify leads and opportunities that merge your ideas with further potential for your working life—heading for growth and success draw advancement into your world. Investing your time in growing your skills attracts rising prospects that crack the code to a brighter chapter. Mapping out a plan and working towards your goals let you climb the ladder and advance your life. Doing due diligence and paying attention to detail enables you to discover your working life's proper role. A systematic, well-planned approach leads to greener pastures.

Being flexible, adaptable, and understanding draws rising prospects into your romance. It shines a light on open communication, and thoughtful dialogues crack the code to a more balanced and prosperous environment for your life. It lets you turn over a new page for your personal life. Deepening and advancing romance lights a path towards improving circumstances. It does bring rising prospects into your love life.

Options are coming that improve the potential possible in your world. It enables you to dive into an engaging chapter of fun and friendship. Life becomes more active and open as you connect with someone who offers companionship. Being open to new people and possibilities helps you redefine what you thought was possible in your social life. It lets you turn a corner and head towards magic and adventure.

The Full Moon in Gemini helps clear the slate by healing sensitive areas that may hold you back from reaching your true potential. Focusing on the basics enables you to adopt a low-key approach to improving your foundations. It draws healing, balance, and renewal. The air of manifestation is working in the background to pull new options into your life. It soon places you at a fantastic advantage to improve your circumstances.

A social aspect offers supportive vibes that draw enrichment into your world. Beautiful symmetry is coming, drawing healing and closure into your world. It brings the energy that is quite therapeutic for your mood as it offers lightness and harmony. It forms the basis of grounded energy to expand your life. Consequently, you head towards an uptick of potential that offers new leads ripe for development. Shedding outworn areas resolves the issues that have limited progress. It cracks the code to a brighter chapter ahead.

You can honor your wild and rebellious tendencies and embrace the path that comes calling. Heeding the yearning within your heart stokes the fires of inspiration. A passionate approach ahead opens to diversity, creativity, and success. It is a journey that unearths hidden gems of possibility. Sifting and sorting through the various options help you come up with a winner. Taking down barriers harnesses the sense of manifestation that offers new territory and an expansive view to contemplate.

DECEMBER

Sun	Mon	Tue	Wed	Thu	Fri	Sat
					1	2
3	4	5	6	7	8	9
10	11	12	13	14	15	16
17	18	19	20	21	22	23
24	25	26	27	28	29	30
31						

December 4th - Mercury at Greatest Elong: 21.3°E

December 5th - Last Quarter Moon in Virgo 05:49

December 6th - Neptune Retrograde ends in Pisces

December 12th - New Moon in Sagittarius 23:32

December 13th - Geminids Meteor Shower. Dec 7th - 17th
December 13th - Mercury Retrograde begins in Capricorn

December 19th - First Quarter Moon Pisces 18:39

December 21st - Ursids Meteor Shower Dec 17th -25th

December 22nd - Yule/Winter Solstice at 03:28
December 22nd - Mercury at Inferior Conjunction

December 27th - Cold Moon. Moon Before Yule. Full Moon in Cancer 00:34

December 31st - Jupiter Retrograde ends in Taurus

NEW MOON

FULL MOON

Neptune retrograde ends in Pisces; it promotes focusing on big sky dreaming. Neptune is associated with creativity, dreams, and magic. Life brims with unique potential. Exploring a variety of interests and pathways reawakens your sense of adventure. You land in an enriching landscape that nurtures creativity and places the spotlight on developing your dreams. Entertaining discussions offer a lively and engaging landscape that encourages happiness and well-being in your life. An emphasis on home life cultivates stable foundations.

Changing priorities may shift your focus to a slower pace that promotes happiness in your life. A social aspect benefits as thoughtful discussions attract unique leads and ideas that nurture an upward trend in your life. Trailblazing conversations lead towards developing new ideas. Sharing discussions with kindred spirits as fuel to your inspiration and amplifies the potential in your world.

Developing your life around the home nurtures a balanced and stable environment. It brings ample time to connect with friends, and improving your circumstances is a significant part of this process. An optimistic outlook places you in alignment to expand your horizons. An invitation ahead hits a sweet note in your social life, bringing a whirlwind of activity that promotes excitement into your world.

The New Moon is in Sagittarius this week, with Mercury going retrograde the day afterward. A variety of factors are at play in the situation with Mercury. Making a move a priority will create a shift forward next year that enables you to build foundations that offer room to progress life forward. A positive trend lets you create space for developing your goals. It shines a light on a productive chapter that enables you to make your mark on achieving a long-held dream. It establishes a passageway towards greener pastures.

Cultivating your creativity adds the fuel of inspiration to your life, which enables you to grow your circumstances and develop your dreams. It helps you promote progress as you create new projects and launch your star towards growth. An upward trend ahead offers room to advance your skills and abilities.

You open the book on a new chapter of potential, information arrives that sparks your interest. Acting on a hunch is wise as you can trust your instincts to guide you correctly towards advancing life forward. New options emerge in your life that gives the green light to connect with self-expression and creativity. The winds of change breathe fresh air into your surroundings. A positive influence lets you dabble in a creative hobby that dials down the stress. It nurtures well-being and offers a balanced foundation that restores and rejuvenates on many levels

Ursids Meteor Shower illuminates refreshing possibilities. Being adaptable and focusing on the bright side nurtures an abundant landscape. It does bring a wonderful time shared with friends and loved ones. A theme of improving circumstances enables you to connect with joy and create treasured memories. It draws balance foundations that will enhance home life. News arrives that brings a boost into your world. It blossoms into an active and lively environment.

New options open a curious path ahead that lets you dip your feet into a new area. It shines a light on social engagement, collaborations, and ambitious endeavors that nurture creativity. Your willingness to explore leads is instrumental in bringing refreshing options into your life. Opportunity arrives and brings a focus on self-development and growth. Any rough edges soon smooth out as you get busy developing your dreams.

A window of opportunity is opening that helps get life on track to head towards greener pastures. Indeed, your journey ahead glimmers brightly with new possibilities. Being open to change facilitates growth and lets you take in unique pathways of learning that improve your life experience. It offers a transition to a more balanced and stable environment that helps you get busy and nurture your dreams. You can cook up a storm and manifest your happiness by focusing on your goals and priorities.

DECEMBER WEEK FOUR

Yule/Winter Solstice at the beginning of the week with a Full Moon in Cancer midweek, followed by Jupiter retrograde ending on the last day of the year in Taurus.

Lively discussions with friends and companions attract a productive and engaging environment. It provides stability and balance that supports a theme of emerging abundance in your life. Curious news arrives that offers insight into the path ahead. Setting goals and developing a plan enables you to grow your world outwardly. Communication arrives that opens the floodgates to socializing with friends and loved ones. It brings a busy time for creating positive outcomes by sharing thoughtful discussions that nurture creativity and unique ideas.

A new influence is looming that underscores unique possibilities of abundance. Exploring a variety of pathways leads to progress, expansion, and good fortune. Building your career path offers a positive trend that connects with higher learning and a chance to grow your talents. You hit the jackpot when you discover a journey that offers advancement and growth. Being a keen observer will help you spot a golden opportunity.

Beautiful changes are emerging around your home and family life. It offers a chance to mingle with people who support your growth and evolution. Connecting with your social life draws an active time of nurturing happiness in your life.

NOTES

NOTES

The one-stop Astro-shop.

https://mystic-cat.com/

Printed in Great Britain
by Amazon

14287344R00071